T0154304

WE ARE NOTHING AND SO CAN YOU

∞

COMMUNE EDITIONS

Red Epic, Joshua Clover
We Are Nothing and So Can You, Jasper Bernes
That Winter the Wolf Came, Juliana Spahr

We Are Nothing and So Can You

JASPER BERNES

∞

Commune Editions
Oakland, California (communeeditions.com)

An imprint of AK Press / AK Press UK
Oakland, California (akpress@akpress.org)
Edinburgh, Scotland (ak@akedin.demon.co.uk)

© 2015 Commune Editions
Second printing 2016
    we encourage the sharing of this book and everything else: *omnia sunt communia*

Cover illustration and Commune Editions design by Front Group Design
    (frontgroupdesign.com)

Library of Congress Cataloging-in-Publication Data

Bernes, Jasper
    We are nothing and so can you / Jasper Bernes

    ISBN 978-1-934639-15-3 (pbk.: alk. paper)
    Library of Congress Control Number: 2014958776

Printed on acid-free paper by McNaughton & Gunn, Michigan, U.S.A. The paper used
    in this publication meets the minimum requirements of ANSI/NISO Z39.48-1992 (R2009)

for the partisans

Foule esclave, debout! debout!
Le monde va changer de base
Nous ne sommes rien, soyons tout!

—Eugène Pottier, "L'internationale"

The thing about things is that they're just gross
totals disguised as taste or caste but no matter
how many times you crank them
backward through the paces of their facture
or go at them with a hammer
you just can't find the switch that lets
the condensates of human toil
start lighting up on contact
as in the music video for *Billie Jean,*
which does not make anyone
into everyone else exactly
unless the future anterior grid
commit such face to flames, the spliced
repeating digits of the rowhouses
as maintain, from behind, the thoughts in citizens
of sixty-five countries mirrored
in the big box store across
the tracks behind the garden, which matters.

That's the thing about things, broken hinge beside the point
we were by halves returned from
having to hack away at the *axis mundi*
with the rough side of a Neolithic sundial.
We are the visitors of such advice.

Something you wipe down with a legal
lights out, a series of superogatory diagnostics.
Our life could be your band.

The products on the shelves, pickled by geometry.
They are our chorus, fourth axis, add to zero.
They set the limits, load the springs, force such place
as nerve and muscle assume the paltriest
infinity of shapes perdition
stamps inside the passbook fantastic.
The red moons of it drag us through each other.
Why is it that the dead have the best propaganda?
Why is what churning now the stern blonde dressed up
to climb such swerves between the blasts?
Accomplices, depleted plants, past the infiltration
complexes and the leaning towers:
the brain, a kind of trading floor, a land
all borders without volume.
That's not an assertion so much as a ruthless
misunderstandpoint loaded up with
epistemological weaponry,
fastened against the approach
of nightfall's legal claim
on unregistered bodies
singing along with the signal flags
carving up the rump-state of Aristotelian physics—
an arrangements of hastenings, finalities,
backfooted claims releases.
Oh, the sad life of the professional
truth-proceduralist! Once the air goes
out of the piety market, you're just there
all blacked out between the collector and the lecturer.
You're a museum, moving upward from the legs and hips
and felonies, the dialectical stank
foreclosing houses, its indentured height which was a place
reflected lengthwise in the mounded, mushroom-headed
fill that blooms at Alcatraz, its algebra of stern and aft
the flowering rebar issued from chunked concrete
our third nature, decanted from the things
impersonal and abstract singing the *Marseillaise*
in trees bedecked with bicycle wheels

and post-human PCP poems.
The product songs dig moats of debt
around the city blocks. A tiny copy inside each object!
To be unselved, unrepossessed, regrafted
fuse, insouciant poof, pursuant to a point of procedure
in that body unable to dissolve, once and for all,
while the wrecking ball of reserve dollars
scatters the primitivists across the internet.
It's sort of a big personification engine —
you suck out the insides of people
you dial ext. 234
you consult the grammar books for the optative case, the everything case,
and *voilà*, you've got an ape that speaks through things, you've got a society
constructed from lots of first-person statements
like "I still died, yo" and "I set up a distribution network to support
combat in an almost infinite multiplicity of places";
"I am some matter"; "I am a shadow cast by everything you do not see"
"I am the nation of no part"; "I am an arrangement of scalar voids
charged with cross-determination."
Like the shadow of fun, there is an app for being drained
from within; there is some coloring done around the edges
which produces a sense of belonging and/or locomotion
by pulverizing the object world into measurable
intervals, blooms, blasts, a ringing in the ears
arranged in advance, arranged to exact
the speed at which one consumes oneself
obstructed by buildings, sidewalks, blurry interiors, machines,
because you cannot beat the dead in a game of patience
and everyone but you and your friends and the people with appendages plugged into
the grid will have been dead,
roe sacs sizzling in bacon fat, roe sacs with master-slave reduction
the eternal rule of the overlords of overshare,
corpse paint and no tempo, roe sacs in collateralized doubt obligations,
the half-completed condos
floating on the bread factory's plinth,
another juiced tweet, another catchment
below the total surface hurt, the shareholders
breaking it down for us, schema of hormones and traffic lights
falling out of finality
like poetry in 1917
reshuffling the natural laws

by putting giant magnets
inside the public offices
rock, dirt, lava
up through the ceiling of consciousness,
the blindsight, the flatline…

A small incision from waterside
then an injection of white people, their likenesses
gradually more intelligible:
lower limit anarchist squat
upper limit wine bar.

History is what [hearts]
curse shared out among the holes in personhood, the cars,
in the twist of torsos, the swing of blood,
a billion and a half tons of plastic and metal
moving around bound to some insane imperative
the stiffening cast of motion, shutter and shadow
morcellized, that's my jam,
that's the molecule won't compute,
won't shut up about how weird it is
no other world is possible
except all of them
superscription of the melancholic
slogans whose freedom is need

Curse shored against the sugared wires, the splintered letters
Life insurance…check
Vasectomy…check
Siphon…fail

Pendulous upendings! A patent on the back,
cash up front, up the nose, down the crotch
behind everything, a privacy w/o equity
attaching the subordinate clauses to the floppy ears,
a little facetime
with the master race. (Note: they look
terrible without their makeup).

Wave hello: that river of references
moving opposite to absolutes

the steel plate in your skull
grinding against the continental
shelf, and where the two collide
a kind of dance party or city of five
million springs up on the Wei river
because it's year zero and the hedges
the sandbags the barricades have
collapsed and now we finally fit into
the size zero dresses, our address is null
and void rogue waves of payment
dunk the Nelson Mandela parkway
automaton of thing-thinging-things
which people hyphenate or sometimes
the malformed stumps of public metals
by dumping the Rand on the open market
wet paperbacks, a stained eviction letter
dollhouse beside a container of cornmeal
it looks like the libertarians got here first
everyone's an abolitionist of some kind or another

To which answer the question is not at all
one of fizzing headphones or the ceaseless
titration of things to things above the broken
link made good by lives split perpendicular
to their own activity a fine narcotic dust
or moral tedium affixing the medial
phrases to the diplomatic servomechanism

held up face-down about the old
slime of established fact, of time consistent,
time incomplete, the papal bull, the laminated
placemat with its double mill
wrestles up the grid we mob, and where no change
occurs, in stereo, at gunpoint, *boing*, pleasantly, by fork and knife
no change occurs.

Briefly, the banal paradoxes of timetravel
shuffle our undead parts through
the pores in the workday, the friction,
the top-heavy narrative, rust and grit
demands impede the transfer of torque

7

and from the wheel of bodies the wheel of money
moves the things that move the bodies
tiny strokes adjust—torpid clock,
measuring its plaids by means of payment
no final destruction vouchsafes.

I never saw the panda punch the cop.

Their tattoos, untranscended, unlock
the little children by the stairs—
the thing is on, we're live from the
server farm on the moon.
Yeah, basically, humanity…a caucus of depressed
apes taped together by the boomerang
of programmable matter, which moves either
slower while the other moves faster, or faster
while the other moves slower and therefore
hurts less or more than bare being.
The zoo is really just one big exhibit:
the N. American Homo Artificialis,
force-fed though the voluble casework
of habit, the simple bonds of the bourgeois family,
to which attach the foodstuffs and trinketized
feelings, the one-point perspective, light
brigade of virgin ontologies, our late display, its salad of malady
piled atop the great misshapen
happening of wealth where the sea was once,
shell-pocked, elective, civilized and critical.
Flames, too, are a form of literacy.

This is where we meet each other
once the cameras have been destroyed,
once the metering of time by hallways and workdays
by which we experience a change of ownership
has been destroyed, and the face deformed by things it has to say, destroyed,
and the diagrammatic metals of combustible elsewheres, destroyed,
and the destruction, destroyed.

There were meetings. There were some things and we met inside or around them. Meetings in daylight, on the tilted lawns, where we let the wind drag our thoughts around a bit. Meetings that pivoted upon a point of discomfort. There was democracy and it was a joke. There was secrecy and necessity. There were mergers and acquisitions and maps with arrows and hardware baptized by the love of almost everything except. There were non-constitutive imbalances. There was the sharing of things and then there was getting stuffed back into our perfectly ruined bodies imperfectly. There was the deep overhang of tedium, fires, shame. There was a them and they thought about it. There was an it and it thought about us, in quotations, in fine, as the normal distribution of planning and chaos on a boulevard at night.

We met the quota. We met the ambassador of sufficient causes in a testing cabin. We met with the children of the enemy. We met the giant structural collapse of the west with a few well-placed kicks. We messed everything up. We made up. We were women sometimes and men other times and no one mostly, and this might have worked out except the other ones left and he thought that he thought, usually, like a me, like going around the edges of stuff was not so rough and besides, the fires sucked up all the tear gas and also consumed the bulk of the solids, stringing them out into characters and regulars of smoke or ways to do things, allegedly. Why shouldn't he stand in that smiling semicircle, with his knees bolted to the precept, while everyone else was changing their money into time? That was analysis, a lasso, unless, absolutely, before the bleeding tower, he remained in a manner the butler of his own foreclosure, a lumpy coil of fatted transistors? Another biosynthetic teatime / two kids using the overturned cop car as a kind of seesaw.

I saw Montmartre. Nothing was on fire, as predicted.
OMG, the universe! Most of it missing!

Where hunger was, the cement of diverse categories
Become the cubes or taking place of an awkward
Relation to the glittering, plastic pronoun
That does its dirty work
Singing Queen on the steps of Sacré-Coeur

And then the headless Lacoste mannequin
Speaks ellipses under fashion, the catacombs, a kind of mall.
Argent urgencies! The skull-and-bones ring
On the wedding finger, clicked twice
Upon the glass of beer, as if to invite
One bridge or another to meet its end
In the new Piranesis of what we no longer
Defend from love, as money,
"A pleasure Cruise…before the whole Human race"

Black flag of the Seine, shaking off the old, civilizing
Bruises. The Square du Vert-Galant
Shoaled upon the outflanking time of time itself
Keel of class its jagged line of advance

Like the Versaillaise over the wall the experiment over
So that now I only get to speak when buying things
Putting some non-simple types of being around stuff
Into hands and short simple phrases compelled by
Violent reciprocity—"General Society," where the monies
Singing each to each open the little window against the moon

The population fizzes in the hazy square
One chant to unite them all

The rising tide will wreck all boats
All votes, their tangled topology, combined

Like, wow, that's *das Man*, that's

Just as ruthless, just as just
As the blunt adjustments forcing the face
Into a shit-input, a slot

For social determinations like
Burning or the bakeries giving out
Free bread at 5 a.m.

We have this little hole in us that secretes truth
Staining the dance floors with
Checkmate and shipwreck

These man-made hills
Of trash, mouthwash, eyelashes
A kind of census
Turned to smoke and ready-to-wear
Incontinence, while
The continental plate grinds out another
Half-hearted civilization the university
Attempts to stitch together
With an epistemological supermajority
Fields of marjoram on fire
On the island of Majorca

In a minor key the looters forced
To throw their guns into the Tiber

Can't you feel it? The flame of reason
Striking coldly on the animal-men
Jutting from the sides of Notre Dame

Offering their names up to the new
And improved cocktails, the declassed
Wharves where the least part of the morning
Rebounds against the tardive piles

"Comparable to a silent expansion or
To the *diffusion*, say, of a perfume in
The unresisting atmosphere"

The zones of ambience and equivalence
Lavished upon the valiant
Aviation of intuitive explode
And now the damages the states of excitation
Tagged with keys to feelings we thought
Settle into invoices in the voice of recording-lice
He didn't think she wouldn't go, they observed.
Were they now nothing, he thought. Or was it simply,
As he should have known then, fumbling for his
Keys on the dark cobblestones of the quai, a tissue of
Usherances, a delayed and yet premature urgency, the wheels
Of the cannon broken by one kick?
LZ is in jail it's horrible now we will have to think
About stuff forever like a computer
The barricades bedecked with painted eyes
Blinded by the real look of things

We had been barricaded inside the Louvre for a length of time you could not measure in time. Sandbags, maybe, or candles. Something gravitational. Or wind, you could measure it with miles of wind unwinding through the galleries. Most of the fighting was in the west, where the lights were on, where the paramilitaries fed on delicacies looted from the markets. At first there had been some fighting on the north side, all the furniture of empire shot to pieces, catching fire. But once we put the fire out, the police were gone. They had run out of bullets or patience or they had stolen all the things they wanted, while we barricaded that side of the museum with the vast, plumed wreckage of the Occident. A few of our number got lost and ended up in Germany or Los Angeles or Japan, and we read about them in the library—we decoded their messages using the guidebooks, the secret geometries, the numbered series of times and places, filtered through violently allusive iconology, and they said that half of the past was coming for us, was against, and that half of the past was coming for us, was for, but lost then in the forest of unbecoming consequences. Et in Arcadia Ego, etc. You could make up little songs about it. Everywhere we went, carved and threaded through the blind stone, the coolly rational waves of stone pushed us forward, pushing the past behind even when it was in front of us, room after room gone dark for good, as if the dark were a kind of combustion, slower than fire but faster than rust.

Every face is a fight, a replacement, traced
Up into lean claims on seeming to
Live out one time by means of another, like a honeymoon
Suite in the lean-to of a zoom lens or color-space
Which strip-mines duration. Its petals dial in
Or so goes the seminar, the incisive airs.

I am not an anarchist, but I'm not afraid
To use anarchy, on TV...One of those sadnesses
Is true, and it makes a door in the smoke
Or a kind of sense—dulled slogans in letters of crystal
Meth competing with the mathematized sunrise
For Most Valued Instrument

Which the web of probes inserting sapient
Commas into the latest report
From the Institute for the Elimination of Whitey
Hurls into sub-orbital elision...

To be unbent into freedom!
To be forever unchanged back into Man or whatever!
Why is it so quiet here on the middle edge
Or were the whites beaten by the red wedge

Into a sad, Himalayan meringue
And now it seems
We'll have to discover something else to use
Our ration books for, like poetry?

I'm just not interested in the Pope. I prefer Prince
And I also prefer the incontestable non-rule
Of the hundred thousand nuclei
Where the party, as stated, no longer
Absorbs the massive and immediate
Staying put of its orbit
But what is it constructs
These destroyers, what terrible humanism
In the overgrowth, what idealism in the mangled timetables?

I face it, like a firing squad faces the sea.

Like the sea faces an old regime of represented beauty.

And beauty, its hateful mirror.

And hate, its boiling truth.

And seeing, its torn seams.

You lived on a graph, by graft.
You were +1, a dotted flight
away from the intersection of GDP
and suicides per year.
Of course there were books
but you were no longer curious
about what lay inside them.
Dust, probably, or specks of sun,
present participles that couldn't not
be arranged into a threat…
The promotion and hospitalization
of attitudes inside the vacuum,
as if you could just turn off the smaller
gravities, or the traffic lights, or…
The wind opened the door
by making a whirlwind in the lock.
They had guns and it wasn't ok.
I mean, aesthetics? Really?
I can appreciate that weird narcotic
gloss on objects as much as the next
person, but I don't think that makes
me worthy of murder. I have facts:
I have lists. I know
exactly how it will go:
up, then up again, then down

They were the unconscious of our unhappiness. This was their bliss, their way of taking the piss. It meant a lot like. They tipped it in everywhere. They had their own frequency, just above the place where, when the older ones were children, the world of free television stopped and the wide fields of cable opened for the few families that could afford it or steal it. Channel 13 was the end of the road, and now, just past there, at 70 cm and beyond, the frames splash on the waves, fast as unthinking...

—You take the end of a car antenna and bend it, just like this; and a screwdriver, you put some tension on the lock, like this...

—The dead are glamorous like that...

—He conducted interviews with their decaying bodies, there. The luster of their skin, its monarchy, just like that...

—Spring, upper pin, lower pin, it looks like this...

—To the frontiers of human experience, their bodies forming a pyre, the dead grown around the base of the living apex...

—Clothes, sea, clouds. Yellow and gray and brown, here and here and here. A severed head, borrowed from a lunatic asylum...

—The tonality of the sea in its empty, rotten sockets, the farce of restoration, see...

—The pins, in their correct positions, clustering like notes on a staff, and you bend the staff, you bend the space the sounds fill, with a click, until they all line up on one ledge, empty

tone, the pure space of hearing, open like a room, like this…

—All of us lived through the restoration, like that. On what raft, like this…

—"I started running like a madman and did not stop until I reached my own room." "Our whole society is aboard the raft of the Medusa."

—Or you could just kick down the door…

—Winds blew so hot they cracked furniture and shattered glasses in the shape of the Mediterranean…

—Oh, my grotesque and craggy melody, I am overrun!…

—Planes real and imaginary, the raft-like tossing of the flattened, depilated shapes and submergences present there, as if bulked up in another dimension we dare not disinter, held together by pins of the most intricate thoughts…

—An immense dossier crammed with authentic proofs and documents of all sorts…

—He took black powder or seedgrains in the hollow of his hand, sprinkled a film of white ones on the top, and said to his Judges, "Behold they are white;" then shook his hand, and said "Where are the Whites? Où sont les Blancs?"…

—And because the painting of the raft is itself a raft, we float it away.

so far I am nearly
beyond getting into

getting down with The Thing

its wings spread on the gulf
between appearing and what breaks

5,000 feet below before the surface

erasing all the sordid after-clarities
about being stood up on two feet

with some ancient irresolvable counterfact

oozing from your ears
while the "sales technicians"

descend from the helicopters

just when we were getting used to being alive
mostly and in fragments

according to a government panel

the great official seals of air on air
closing out necessity and the tangle of streets

how a failure became an option
topped off with torn-to-pieces.
Capitalism — how does it work?

a matrix of acts, inexact, x-ed out

and undercounted, overruled, compelled
to become a sum that never dawns

a sun whose blacks twixt past and future

mount a series of tactical strikes
in the precise place that body is no body

and therefore matters, is the keep of the real, the reaper's keel

They are there is. We are were or will. It's a big blur, whispery and once-upon-a-time-ish. The man next to you is holding a gun, it really is a gun, it's pointed up at the dead sky and toward some hateful unseen star about to go supernova though the light won't reach us ever, there's too little or the wrong kind of it, and then it makes a noise, the gun does, that seems to come from that far away. The sound is like the snapping of something manufactured to never break, not ever, manufactured at the molecular level, like the refutation of all ontology, and now the police line breaks, the police are running, they are out of formation and sprinting, their batons striking out of time, striking the people unlucky enough to be that close, and for a while it's as if you're inside of the same body as the police, as if they are a predatory growth inside some body or you are, in flight, from what you or they were like, furious cell division, combustion, scarring, blood, circulation, you're knocked down and picked up and running and tripping over another body that is your body that is hostile or friend you can't tell, you're slammed into a wall, and the wall gives, and you're up and running again you can barely see anything, the ground is giving way and painted lights are coming up from the ground, they hit you in the face like a breathable foam, the colors seeping through the darkened canvases.

The categories, made by right to walk
crab-wise across the rope bridge,
shot at from above and below
by a real idealism, an abstract
monster of measurement, neurotransmitters
synced with metal and stone
with flowers of muscle and bone.
Articulate, many-voiced whips!
The grasses and trees
flash on the dumb pond
poisoned by a thought.
We move through the sewer system
gingerly, sketching on the underside
of the surface of the world
a map of the city to come, with brackets
holding in place the things we can't
begin to begin being
perhaps because we were
unwilling to count ourselves
among the things of the world
or perhaps because we did.

Either you take sledgehammers
and alienate the eternally-
deeded marbles of the one true church,

the hacked-off chunks, tossed at
police lines in aerial
high relief, or you use them as
a backstop for your failing
war currency, its value rising and falling
like the blades of a guillotine
as if without the state's
monopoly on violence
the objects of the world
would blow away like
tumbleweeds, leaving us free forever,
the Footlocker on Broadway boarded up
once again, as the narrowing remains
hit the switches—

and if a whole nation were
to feel ashamed it would be like
a lion recoiling in order to spring

Well, it was enough. There were theories about us. The River continued to jockey for position, but The Cloud was everywhere, and no individual member could understand, at first, what they had initiated. It was just a simple image, a shape even, but in its slight displacements, its balances, suggestions, no one could resist snapping a picture of it with their phones, putting it up on the internet, sending it to friends. It was the face of same, the acting on itself of same. And no one could resist it because everyone knew it. Where the painted walls stamped themselves against the air, they applied silver burnished in such a way that natural air and sky were reflected in it, and even clouds that one saw pass by in this silver, pushed by the wind, when it was blowing, were ensnared thereby. We were time out of mind, and this meant the machines were not our defended memories but our way of feeling out along the edges, for once, like a slow leak in ending up alive around the subroutines, the points computable and not, the radical chains of irregular distributions of past times which would not come off. And so the machines shut down—for 30 seconds, or a minute, or 5 minutes, or 3 hours. And then they started back up. And then shut down again. This was the discourse the master taught, the cold shock of the void. This was the point, falling capriciously and cruelly from the sceptered towers of the city. Without the mobile or stationary screens, the flow of images and figures across our eyes, what were we, what did we owe to this place? When the lights went off, nothing was owned. There was nothing to do and we did it.

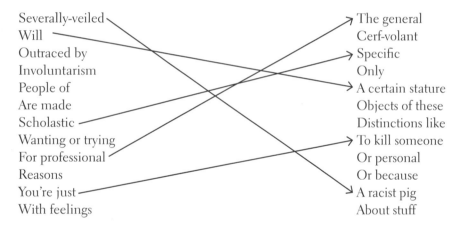

Severally-veiled The general
Will Cerf-volant
Outraced by Specific
Involuntarism Only
People of A certain stature
Are made Objects of these
Scholastic Distinctions like
Wanting or trying To kill someone
For professional Or personal
Reasons Or because
You're just A racist pig
With feelings About stuff

Are not these our properties?
The sad passions, sapped by a system of weights and measures?
Some hate takes and some hate breaks.

Looted fitteds fly through the air,
As if we were graduating
Into the terrifying unrelatedness
Of these things and bodies
As if a bank were just brick and glass and paper
Animated by an archaic, insane script.

26

But now that we know that every
Atom of the world is outfitted
With a tiny extradimensional camera

What use can we have for remembering
To die here and there 30 times per second?

I'm sure my nonchalance will rescue yours
Wearing some kind of decorative trauma

But now the white baby stroller
Emerges from the fog

And we start to run

Surviving off the continuous passage of its moment of realization, transferred, hall by hall, like the angel of death above the marked doors of the Israelites, a tone blown-out to mere topos. Humanity thus inevitably sets itself only such tasks as it is able to convert into a series of off-on switches. It took us months. We were meticulous, replacing every pair of eyes in every painting or figurine or sculpture with a 0 or 1, with love or hate, life or death, truth or falsehood, labor or capital (the content hardly mattered); replacing the genitals with transistors; the mouths with capacitors; the whites and yellows with fine arrays. It was almost ambiguous, in the river, our genders awash. It was our Sphinx, our blighted remind. It made the whole history of art into time that answered its own question — like, why is there something instead of nothing? And when will we finally win? How much is left? It reduced to Tokyo to Ok, New York to New, Paris to Is. 19 20 21. But since it answered only with light or sound it required a myth to be explained. This won't be that myth.

The times of things describe the circle
"He was raised by wolves"
"And Swedish au pairs"
"And a dark cloud whose
Intercommunicating vapors…"

The times of things avant la unbecoming
Whimper at the scabby heart of the matter,
Decentered carousel of hand and eye
There is a new version available
Whose tangents describe
The turning spit of sovereign abstraction:
An hour is an hour is our
Face planted in bright dirt and.
The red thread of lived activity
Woven into white ticking
And stretched across the sky
Until the smolder and suffer of bildung
Removes the ding-dong from the dull
Bells of arrival and we use the buildings
As giant bongs or Mao Zedong
Machines or medial
Porquería, time not as translation
In space but height or falls

Above the slough and thrill
Of discontinued parts
Let x let yet, let y let then, let all
The knotted, wrung-out, loveless
Rates decoct as crystal and as crisis
All that rises without at

Or would we? Were we not the ones who—in the swerves and gaps of history— transform general will into a kind of general was, into the dailies and rushes of counterfact, the epic fail, man-nation? Or would the 500 years experiment find at its limits not just capitalism or class society but the human form, not just the speaking ape but all the carbonated sacs of self-reproducing logos that foamed out of that old, terrible constancy? You stood stupidly in the field. Your brow was like the focusing ring of a camera—you could tighten it around a tiny color and the foreground would flow back into a kind of low tide of the mind where the old oppositions seemed to dissolve, lengthwise, heightwise, now-wise, into the non-identity of cell and circuit. Would it have been meaningless, then—the communist impulse, invariant baseline of those final human centuries, banished and expelled, crushed and restructured and dusting the bedsheets of the hospital ward, yet still arising, again and again, with all its clamor and naming? Shouldn't we have simply hastened on the end, cheered on the hot, whirring metals of the computers in the basement? The frequencies collecting in our forehead did feel good—we understood it not at all at once, the bright reasons flashing like stairs in the dark. We drank it up. And then we fought as hard as we could.

Waveshaping on overdrive
Every time I don the black mask
Or whip my hair back and forth
And other poems
Among the sealed rewards
And vacuum-tube effects
Or the sweep of the basin
Overtaking the flan
Or dude's at it again
Fuck, shark's fin soup…
Streaming live from the bookfair
An experiment in collective annihilation
In my financial crisis suit
And gemeinschaft gels
And reconfigured institutional logic
Or often just too detached
From the background
Funding model for
How can I join one more
Committee where I can do
Something useful like
I was just frontin'
Whose cause was man
But now just then

We came to the clearing among the semiconductors
Or each of us the treasurer of our own currency
Or we have only tragedies in common
Emplotting the crater left by the sublimation of the gods
Or the rare minerals able to blast us back
Sleep by sleep

We were, like, martyrs but smarter. We just pretended to suffer. All of the snitches had logical operators tattooed on their backs. The rest of us huddled in the corner, like propositions. Slab, we yelled. Slab, slab, slab. Even with such a rudimentary language, you could calculate the stitchwork by which the snitching meant we fell or stood at the same time, together. Slab, etc. We were fucked. Slab slab slab.

Which ones, we learn, are wasted
as much as they are any ones, any zeros,
plasticine ejaculate of empty time,
preterite of futures
fashioned from useful idiocy
and rotted vegetables,
then exported into a historical landscape
in which every unrecovered cash
payment harries the pilgrims
as they go around the desert places
collecting campaign buttons.

Because even an internal enemy has its internal enemy, etc.,
and wrecks as result the sad dream of clear
decision sweeping through the bodies
bloodlessly, without anyone losing even one finger
to the contradiction…

Look! The placement of squares on a sphere
and the placement, moreover, of bodies in the
squares on the sphere,
like a sea in storm,
end to end so it's over or all over
for those fuckers whose viral cogitation

means that we purchase back what
little remains of us
after the weekend.

Violence cut with grace!
Shaved Brussel Sprouts with Pancetta and Marcona Almonds!
A long string of conjunctions and prepositions
like ball bearings sliding around inside the sentence
to keep the bloated nominalizations
from catching on fire as they obliterate
everything around them
like the feelings which from psychic ordinals
collide on an infant's face.

I alone hold the key to the narrow wilds…
And I will make the people pass through one by one.
I will make death pass through also
at random like the atoms in one of those things
I was.

Because there were more rules than there were things, many more, countlessly more, because, indeed, the rules made little whirlpools of infinite abandon inside the things, which seemed removed the more they seemed ruled, and because everyone and everything seemed to have its own rule, its own disenchanted genius, so that no one could really be said to be ruled at all, if rule then meant a domination we shared. Because anarchy, in other words, and each of us slated to suffer a unique violence, a violence like a name, with nothing general about it. Some thought this meant that communism was already here. Others thought it meant communism was impossible, since we would never be able to match up the electrical flares in our brains with the patterned inertia we encountered. But wasn't that the point – the unworkable?

At least we were tired of "it" —whatever "it" was—tired of rehearsing, under the rotting awnings, a few moments of unverified intimacy from the last hours of the little credit we had left. Was that seriously what was meant by art, after all the bandages had been removed? We had burned all the banks by the sea. Ours was not a normal darkness. Not, in other words, the darkness of shadow, of obscuration, light blocked by solids. No, ours was a radiant darkness. It spread out from our skin like any shining except that it cancelled shine. Dragged into the clearing at the heart of all hell breaking loose, it fled from us and into the stars. Kicking through the liquid crystal displays into the musty rooms of pimply middle-class adolescents intent on bringing down the government for reasons no one could articulate, because all articulation is, in fact, raison d'État, a red herring at best. The most you can do is trick it out to fit the limits of your particular human organism, its mangled sensorium.

We get an old city bus and give it the number of a line that doesn't exist—47 or 810. Immediately we exclude all those sad characters who know where they are going and want to go there, who think in terms of means and ends, origin and destination, or who are compelled to do so for reasons of material or perhaps moral circumstance. This narrows our range of riders less than you might imagine. Indeed, we estimate that at any one moment fully one-fifth of all passengers are there for reasons other than the desire to get somewhere in particular. People who could care less where the bus is going, as long as it's going. People whose bodies are exhausted and just want a place to sit down. Kids who are more interested in each other than anything else and who follow with collapsed heads the colored signscape of the world. People who carry their faces in their hands. People who carry things in plastic bags. People who carry other people.

Eventually we have so many buses running, so many constantly improvised lines, and so many partisans running into and out of the buses and grabbing provisions off the shelves of corner shops, with or without guns, and taking the gas that we need from the gas stations, with or without guns, with or without leaving behind the mutilated corpses of police, and getting off one bus and onto another, that the buses become like the rooms of a disarticulated mansion, whirling through space and crossing and recrossing, combining and disassembling in a stupid, manic dance. Some buses are entirely dedicated to sleeping and some to eating, some buses are 24-hour dance parties, and on some buses people bicker constantly. There are theoretical buses and flirtatious buses. There are sanitation buses and fully armed bank-robbing buses and buses that hate all the other buses. There are so many of these buses spinning through the city that, eventually, it truly is as if they were themselves the only thing stationary in a crazy world jumping about in every direction, as if space had too many dimensions to be space but not enough to be time.

In London they make it /
                French in Greece in different
    Voices make it rain /
                Location on vacation
Like all the Puerto Rican /
                Barricades reroute
    The roads to Rome /
                You can blockade them
    From home by remote /
                Control scramble the traffic
    Signals make it January /
                In July in Oakland
Billy's in the Nazi Room /
                Klare's in the loading dock
      In the US they /
                Still make money in China
They can make anything /
                Take time
    By combination of parts /
                Made of making do we can't
    Make out the places on /
                The map they've made
      Dark in daylight /
                In time for New York

To sink behind the paywall /

                    The lake of ink the make and model

      Scaled up to circle /

                  The squares forever

          To drown /

                  The crowds in open skies

By summer's end, we learn much later, no one could agree about when the disturbances began. A dozen years ago, last year, earlier this month: visitors to that part of the city were likely to hear a different answer each time they asked. Anti-riot agents coated every surface of the zone, dulling the green of the trees; the sharp sweet smell of the gas residue was the first thing you noticed once you crossed the river, and some residents suspected these chemicals were the cause of their newfound incapacity with time. In the cafés, impromptu philosophers sat among the shattered tables and chairs, debating whether calendar time even applied in the zone. The riots were rather like the lunar rhythm of the tides, they said, or the layering of weather on weather that formed a climate, spreading through the interconnected neighborhoods as heat diffuses through a block of metal. Indeterminacy in time was offset, however, by the fixed position of the zone in space, skewered by the pushpins stuck in a hundred police maps. Walk a couple of miles in any direction and the calm was absolute — more terrifying, by contrast, than the worst night of wooden bullets and water cannons: the curbs shining with brightly painted color coding, the asphalt as smooth and lineless as a baby's face, affable citizens queuing up in front of the cupcakeries, shaking hands as they greeted the bland regularity of another day. And it was not just the immediate environs: large parts of the country seemed pacified, docile, bright and crimeless and tediously polite. The radius of pacification was spreading day by day, as the national newspapers reported. There were theories, of course, that the rioters were simply the nocturnal avatars of well-behaved citizens from beyond the zone, but none of the photographs could match faces with existing records. Some suspected that deviants from other parts of the country were being deposited in the zone; there were rumors about secret flights, nocturnal renditions, people with cloth sacks over their

41

heads being marched across the bridge. If this were true, the government put up a good show. Entire universities were devoted to studying the phenomenon, developing new weapons and police tactics. Clergy descended on the zone; billions of dollars were funneled into non-profits to address the sources of the disturbance; governmental panels met continuously for the better part of a year, a decade, a century. But then one afternoon toward twilight, while the drones congregated above the river, an elderly man came out from the apartment blocks and, instead of beginning to gather the loose rocks and bricks into a pile, lay down among the debris and went to sleep. Soon another old man came out and he lay down as well. Eventually, the whole neighborhood was there, in the street, parents and grandparents, friends and cousins, lying together in a big pile as if they had expired happily. Nothing happened that night in the zone, nothing was lit on fire, nothing smashed into little pieces; there were no angry declamations, no projectiles. The zone was the calm eye of a storm whose scale was orders of magnitude larger: for thousands of miles in all directions, city after city swept up in the outcry.

And then went downtown
Disguised as minor characters
Who find no end of objects
Turning space to price.
They have named something after you,
Another gaunt outlet chainsawed through solid
Paraphrase, the blunt force of not trying to hear
Scattered in lines and arcs like labor time
Evaporating in a riot.
I step out of the hotel and into the last of all possible worlds.
What reason could I possibly give?
When the lights turned back on, every inch of the city
Tagged up with inequalities

As if again assigned to the burning system of piecework
Let out to the black mass of just-in-time execution
While you navigate the transcendental loop
Athwart overturning a cop car as art
And doing it where the bad neighborhood of real life
Abuts the state. Like everything that shits on you
Consistently, a question of timing.
That's what the state is, in the end—
An appointment book with a gun,
The days stamped onto the metropolitan

Superfice, an entire choreography of dates whose purpose is to schedule
Other dates when one's confinement to a point in space
Cut deep into time
Will be decided.

You lost your way in the teargas one night.
Out of the burning places and back into the catacombs
Of endless work and talk, the ranked textures colliding with the force
Field emitted from the traffic lights
To produce notions of value and utility.
No wonder you just say fuck it and do something really sketchy
Or go to graduate school or get into building bikes.

As again the vats fill up with blood, with our blood
And again the amphibious thing
Crawls out of the Victorian prose
And gets all up in our face:
A mass of bloodied paperwork
Become a viscous pulp, from which limbs
Emerge, then trunks, then heads, then: the police,
Army and postal service all in one.

It's not not believing that maims
But believing in not believing
As if it were a dim anchor
Extruded from the neutral hiding places,
As if you didn't just live here.

The wrongness of words is a wrongness of worlds. This much, at least, we could say plainly, while the poets effervesced around us, scampering into the exacting receivership of the night. We were not poets any longer. We were terrorists. We had graduated, finally, into the stinging light that strikes the isometric pictographs like a death ray strikes the mirrored faces of the robot lords. Standing there in the antechambers, still dripping from that sea of slanderous predicates, armed only with the hollow of the clocks, the massing and tilting of things said by people to the rooms that encase them—we put every last word we knew on paper. We had no choice: the machines took the words from us outright, frontally, like lesser nobles deeding the mowing meadows of the ancient peasantry to themselves, took even the words we tried hardest not to think, took them and translated them into the poetry of the state, the case file, the database. We were expressed, like the juice of a fruit, and that was our last poetry, our final overflowing into the barf bag of total administration. There was nothing left in us but sight, and nothing left to do but see it.

We found the right words once, long ago, the Orphic panorama shuddering with vowels and glossy fire. It was as if anybody was everybody, anywhere everywhere, spread across the whole world, become horizon, threshold. Gimme the fucking money! All of those people crawling around on the ground as if they were collecting tiny fragments of some precious, panic-trampled thing. Gimme the money! Like magic, it made the blood come out of their ears. It made them give up everything that could be seen. As if you were a flame, wicked through the streets of the city, through buildings, through the flaring nostrils and wires and the branches of trees and blades of grass and tangled roots. And yet you knew, at once, that the world with which you were consubstantial

45

was the wrong world, however much the words really did drape down around it like a fitted sheet. Its graduated approximations, its shaped dirt and concrete and steel, its spooling, entropic way of talking to itself about us, its possessed citizens with their calculable transactions and commercial pleasantries and exchange of elaborately printed slips which directed their behavior according to simple arithmetic. Well, maybe.

Life in the metropolis has made me desperately literal, I'm afraid. The things that are true are the things that happen, that keep happening however grandly we refuse to believe in them. They declare themselves outright, as simple as a giant Santa Claus on fire, the walls of the party headquarters puffed out in front of the blast wave.

■

Here there is space and space and space but no time, no dying, not even one nanosecond left for the decay of excited carbon into speculative melodrama from philosophy dudes. So much space you can't move. The surplus oxygen makes the air swim. The light heals over or sinks to the bottom; attenuated people clump together in the damp heat while the objects through which one recognizes them (as us) bulge around you, like the gummy, unblinking surface of an eye. Without time, space hardens, it scabs over, its joints stiffen and its fibers contract, splintering into a scintillant powder. We put on our facemasks. We lean into our tasks.

In a shipwreck there is opening, there is depth, the clearing of the abyss, the cold antisky of the sea. Here, rather, nothing floats. The debris coils around us like a suffocating cast, a constrictor, and those of us who survive, in clumps and piles, do so because of our proximity to the structural supports, the braces and frames that create little air pockets inside the infinitized rubble. To think. To be. To know. We dig in a direction, any direction, and if two or three of us can find each other, we say, then perhaps we can claw a few others out from under the collapsed sub-basements, establish a new cell, a cluster, a supercluster even. Except that the rubble, in this case, is not only inorganic matter; it is other people, the indifferent ones and the antagonists, the betrayed and the traitors. Some of them ground down to pulp and some of them encased in a weaponized exoskeleton. The ones who are too drunk with insipid bloodlust to even move anymore and the ones who nose forward, grimacing, into the spray of brain and guts. Click click click.

Space, then, as the nerve-fractured array whose surface rhythms the world-makers craze into pseudosubstance, shattered and melted down by the continual overwriting of autodevelopmental deep time, the nano-tooled titanium watches encrusted, intricately-geared and lubricated with the years of deadening work the people who made them dusted themselves down around, a kind of programmable rubble, the people who mined, smelted, hauled, unloaded, typed, poured, coded, decoded, sketched, swept, calculated, painted, wiped down, boiled and sold, days squeezed into the deformed equalities, the dazzling pendant things and mannequined suits containing whole towns, days and nights entire, of toil. You could walk down Fifth Avenue and feel it buzzing and pushing in on you, swarming, fighting its way out of the jeweled displays, the textiles, the smells and tastes and sounds in which how many proletarians have drowned—ten thousand? one hundred thousand? one million?

It took a few tries, but eventually we found a host that could smuggle the attack code down to the lowest layer of chips, the lesser deities of the electronic world, the kitchen gods of programmable control logics which run lighting systems, elevators, stop lights, alarms and surveillance cameras. We watched on our screens as the mosaic of sprinkler systems came online in the empty form of the network, the contagion, the curtain we mistake for stage.

Flood, then rainbow. And between them, the crowd of looters who were both roiling sea and surviving ark. Even now, this many years later, I am told that beyond the first wall almost everyone you meet will be wearing a gold watch, a silk scarf, a designer suit.

■

Today, the citizens are everywhere. Swelling the schools and hospitals, the post offices and town halls. All of the places we occupied last winter, where we distributed food and information and read out each day the list of the murdered, whose roofs we had defended with petrol bombs and bricks, whose halls sang out with the sudden inevitability of defeat, as the frowning semicircle of provincial cities were pacified by great clouds of sleeping gas, by buckshot and torture. Now, all these places, every last one, contract, squinting in the terrible, individuating glare of property and state. The people enter them as citizens and not partisans, as countable bodies. One person, one vote. One and one and one, equaling one, no matter how varied the pluralism of candidate and cause. The ghastly monism of the State: a thousand vortices open to the same crushing interior. It sounds like suffering for a reason.

The expansion of the electorate meant a transformation in the machinery of voting. First the introduction of standardized secret ballots printed with special inks on special stock—in other words, the conversion of the ballot into currency—displaced the older, personalized system of sworn voice voting (administered by judges) which could take place only within the demographic limits of white, landowning men. The entrance of heterogeneous populations into the electorate required a homogenization of the electoral machinery, a system in which the process as such votes for itself and we enter as mere relay of momentum, as reflex action, pulling levers, punching holes in paper, tapping buttons which allow for the passage of charge from one tiny dark area to the next. But the machinery under discussion here is more than the particular apparatus in question—the paper ballot, the Diebold machine, the Hollerith cardpunch. I refer instead to a vast counterinsurgency of diffusion, telecommunication, excitation, diversion, postponement and deferral, in which people are asked to invest all of their political desires and needs into the electoral process at the same time as they are forgiven, under the logic of the excluded middle, all responsibility for its consequences.

Since they submit to these mediations so blithely, the citizens, why not make them visible, the way we are visible to each other, as the planetary extension of the epic love affair that so terrifies the tiny-minded rulers? Why not make it so that when the lever is pulled in Ohio, a cop car explodes in New Jersey, a drone crashes into a mountain in Waziristan, the stock market hemorrhages money, a website goes down, this paper bursting into flame?

finally, our faces fail
the smile scanners

the *Ideal* X, clicked and dragged
onto the slimy beach

air warring with air

while the cops impound
Anarchopanda's head

and the new performing arts
complex gets worked up
into bulbous, overbearing slabs

in the dead lot
adjoining the jail.

they used to make cigarettes there

but since we began transitioning to
a James Franco-based mode of production
there are much simpler paths

to suicide: laser light shows,
various forms of participatory
musical theater which convert

to unpaid internships
having other people's
refractory feelings

the party of #yolo clashing with the
party of #reason

on the plain of Agincourt

the gamification of Thatcher-is-dead
piñata parties, neuroresponsive
bundles appropriate for

simple commercial or military applications
Grade AA starting at 7 cents per watt

■

basically, you have three choices:
jail, mall, museum
whose hapless invariance
repeats as edges leaping
away from each problematic

crossing to defeat
all possible reply.

jail + museum =
university; mall + jail
= airport; mall + jail
+ museum = home sweet home

the arrival from which
by mail of that self
called to account by standard

deductions on municipal violence
brings little solace, at last,

and actually there are only
shipping containers, for the most part,

the real x of fungible matter
merges into the keystream

of new products 3D-printed
from vats of pink, pseudopodial slime

while we cower behind
the piles of mortuary stone
left over from the days

when the dead stayed in their graves
when their faces could be told apart

from the smiling living

At the crossroads, the compass fails. Dawn from all directions—at noon, at midnight. The agitated particles of sand spin in place, painted in flower colors by the fugitive auroras. Aerosolized, they form a gauzy sea, fold on fold of stinging grit through which the half-shapes flicker in quarters and eighths, decocted slowly into the brittle silhouettes of arrivants, alone or in small groups, alone or in pairs, alone or maybe not at all. They arrive in rickety pickup trucks hauling trailers woven from wicker. They arrive with mule teams dragging 40-foot shipping containers. They arrive in city buses filled with grain. In caravans of converted bicycles whose wheels turn the heavy axles of freight cars loaded with scrap iron and salt.

There are two giant warehouses—NOT AND and XNOR—whose terraced, curvilinear interiors swell with shifting mounds of bolts and ball bearings and vats of pickled cabbage. Also: transistors, scarves, batteries, beans, toothpaste, bags of cumin and pepper and salt, textbooks, toys and waterclocks. Superabundances from each of the 500 towns and zones to the west and north and south. Everything that can't be discharged internally or among neighbors ends up here, available to any and to all, because what finds no place in satisfaction of direct or indirect want must remain in motion until it becomes useful. The flows cross but are never exchanged thing for thing, object for object. All the free lands are cut by this simple, unreciprocated distribution of excess, flowing from zone to zone like flocks of migratory birds. Beneath the lake, conveyors carry the goods from the receiving warehouse NOT AND to the much-larger distribution facility XNOR where they are sorted, inventoried, and listed in the databases.

This was one of the first depots to emerge from the revolutionary wars. It was used, originally, as arms stockpile and supply point for partisans who did not fight in order to create communism at some far-off date but for whom the construction of communism, immediately, without compromise, was itself the war. The elaboration of zones like these—places where anyone could take what they needed—was an offensive rather than defensive act, and more powerful than blowing up a bridge or a munitions factory, though that happened too. You can still see the battlements lying around in the middle distance, and this explains, perhaps, the somewhat heavy-handed design of the depot, constructed by people who were born in and had lived decades under despotisms of all sorts, under the boot of wage and market, and who carried these things in them, they felt, as one carries a disease in remission. Literalists of the revolution, then, whose penchant for austere and humorless redundancies of design was held back, thankfully, by the modest range of their power.

Between the two hangars, there is a vast lake in the shape of an X, symbolizing bluntly the void between taking and giving. At its narrow point, a bridge crosses the lake, a bridge itself crossed by an island also in the shape of an X, blinking in the solvent mists whose fragrances pry each thing away from its concept. Some people come only to give and some people come only to take, but those who would make the perilous passage from giving to taking, dark corridor manned in the past by the armed guards of the state and the paralyzing abstractions of value, now must pass directly through this island of variegated singularities, in which the names of all the items available to desire swarm and scroll in anagrammatic collisions and are thereby emptied of all meaning by the multiplying rifts of a field of pure grant and receipt.

The depots also serve another function. Beyond directing objects and necessaries to their final home, they redistribute those persons who have come to feel, in one way or another, in excess of their place in the world. The restless ones, the adventurists. Each depot features a giant mausoleum-like building set off from the others, on a hill or hidden in the woods, inside of which computer terminals list the names and pertinent details of the people who have come here and relinquished their identities, swapping them out for another. Deposit boxes contain other items associated with the donated identity—written testimony, videotapes, bundles of memorabilia and other effects. There is, of course, no compulsion to draw from the available store of identities in leaving one's own behind; one might instead invent an entirely fictive self, a past without past. In fact, in some areas it is a popular pastime to invent such lives and forward them to the depot for listing. All personae are, of course, entirely provisional, and there is no requirement that one keep the new biography for any length of time. This means that fully half of all people will try out a new identity at some point, even if most will return to their old selves sooner rather than later. In some areas, it is an essential rite of passage to leave oneself behind for a few months.

There are many legends about these proteans, especially in the older zones where identity-swapping is more common. In one, a man encounters his former self during a seasonal rotation out to assist with the harvest. This former self, a woman, had committed great atrocities during the wars of revolution, and in most cases such an identity would remain in the depot for eternity, too awful for adoption. There are certain saintly people, however, who purposefully seek out the worst identities of all and strive to develop from them lives of great significance and intensity, returning them to the identity-heap transformed. The woman that the man had previously been had subsequently been so returned, and so accepted by another wanderer who had added to the great significance and intensity of this once unbearably awful life experiences of additional intensity and significance. Because of this, the man fell in love with the woman he had once been, and the two of them travelled together past the boundary lines and into the war places, where they gave counsel to those who would eventually commit great atrocity in some nameless battle or another. They were ignored, of course, and so the nearest depot was flooded with hundreds of lives few people would ever adopt or think about much at all.

Manned by remote, the owl of Minerva, quivering in aspic.
The end of analysis, or California.
It's easier to imagine management, suction, the scaled appeals, light teasing.
Quickly, the passage from potty training to mercantilism.
Price signals cresting the foliage, in Apache gunships.
Jesus is really going to fuck you up, Bunny.
The little love god, stapling the invoices.
It's not just capitalism that I hate.
It's every heretofore existing mode of production.
Beginning with the subordination of mitochondria to the central cell.
I am friends.

The clouds bronze and plummet to earth
Leaving, upon dissipation, an enticing crater
Around which the play of delinquent faculties
Settles into fine, reticulated trails for riding dirt bikes.
Like that, we mourn our carpet burns.
Lurid interregna: a set-theoretical focus group is no politics.
Just think of me as a really incompetent attorney.
Those walls crumbling like a putrid cheese. The air hard with dots.

Fountainhead of all insane forms
Whose foaming efficiency
Circles the surplus populations

Bought on the margin,
Pooled and rolled and written-though and stratified
Unequal to itself, which oceans part
The classifications, antagonisms, insured
Bearers and heirs to a claim on our feelings
About the claims on things
Backed by Bradley Fighting Vehicles and Predator Drones.

In our heart of hearts, hands up.

Our speech was weak. It could not link to the things it liked. Its numbered fucks to give formed a low relief along the centerline. Not that anything was beneath us, poorly formatted as we were, a pile of atomisms and half-formed hellworlds, a whimpering patina poured into the sagging chaise, where we read Low-Intensity Warfare for Everyone on our cracked tablets. We had been socialized by nature. We were wild about it.

There were only two seasons left in the year—revolt and repression; an unruly flourishing of hope and then eleven months of groaning misery in caves. Mostly we tried to sleep. Weeds grew out of the sea, knitting together into ghastly raiding vessels that skidded up onto the beaches, staffed by what the few people to have survived such encounters will describe as a kind of sentient fungus. There were goats everywhere. Grasses spread like wildfire, overgrowing the roads in a matter of hours, then disintegrating in the sudden windstorms.

We spend most of the first night watching a painted spider crawl across the dead screen. Moonlight floods the mineshaft and we look at each other in horror, blinking. As if alongside and external to ourselves, the categories we'd been forced to inhabit, ugly hotel rooms, baroque interest rate swaps, nuanced shades of lipstick, the big rocks ground down into small rocks and the small rocks into pebbles and the pebbles into dust from which, finally, a second, third, fourth or $n+1$ nature could be reconstituted, after the addition of water and sand? Another herd passed, stripping the land of all greenery. I could see the cursor of the wily fiend blinking here and there among the slag heaps.

The problem, of course, is that the supply chains which fed our enemy also fed us; our machines had produced a world wherein we could survive only as accompaniment to our machines, and even then perhaps only by permission. Some of the more egalitarian lifeforms seemed poised to do well—lichen and jellyfish and bacteria, the proletarians of the food chain, fizzing in the hot oceans from which all complex life had departed, spores thickening the acrid, birdless air.

We could feel ourselves receding into the acres of printed matter, the wine-dark twilight. It was all a bit too perfect. Wasn't this all most likely the hallucination of a particularly loathsome and yet influential collection of people who we might track down and encourage to cease thinking immediately, to take it all back, everything, except us? Until then we would make do with the narrow strip of freedom that looped, dizzyingly, through the inhuman foreground, parallel to all particulars.

Perp-walked through the dead mall

the Vandals, Goths, Visigoths, Ostrogoths, Huns
of West Valley Junior High

scrolling helplessly through their contact lists
available weapons
spells

while the tariffs
pummel the technology park.

Elsewhere, what's-her-name fianchettoes her glass
of Sauvignon Blanc

then flings it at the weathered Director of Marketing
whose perverse enthusiasms brought ruin to all.

The dead pixels perforate the scene,
letting the mood leach away into the recent past,
where it's converted to literature.

The balloons go up above the besieged city
carrying to the provinces
the bizarre serial of our freedom, alive
beyond all entangling mediations.

Most are blown out to sea, however
and we spend the next century

hiding on the shadow side of the moon
waiting for the phosphorus to run out
and cheering on our children as they shoot

bottle rockets at the drones.

The freezing, star-lit craters will vouchsafe
the truth about people, perhaps,
after the surviving bacteria once again
evolve new and probably more horrible
forms of intelligent life, wrung
from the song-crushed atmosphere

that keeps the infinity of counterfactual universes
from surging across the interdimensional Bosporus
like looters rushing a supermarket.

If you're reading this it's not too late.

There are no sides. There are aspects and angles, stocks and flows, levels and rates. Faceless volumes flooding the neighborhood. The read-write head, hissing as it slides along the tape. The front is a mood, a surface without standing, an absolute eyesocket, bottomed up. By which we mean, mostly, getting shot at by the architecture. Either that or filleted in an alley by the public good. The buyer visits Detroit, Toledo, Cincinnati, Buffalo; then Toledo, Detroit, Buffalo, Rochester. The Amazon picker grabs an umbrella at A45, a sewing-machine at F38. Folded back with a single twist, the interior of the cylinder becomes its environment. The barricades let the enemies in, then funnel them up to the surface. From there the uniformed schoolchildren in the gray apartment blocks will swiftly stone them to death. The brute-force search, given infinite processing power, will return in historical time the whereabouts of the child-god. Such power, however, is available only on feast days at high noon, and only for half a second. We have therefore managed to survive and even thrive in the polymorphic voids between worlds, preparing our final assault. Below the broken flyovers of the freeway interchange, tunneling through the decision-space left by the collapse of the periodic table. The colonel examines the insignia carefully, its knotted marks uncoiling into a fissiparous clump of red insects that perforate the vault. What is the thing whose insides are our landscaping, bearing upon its flowering shoulders the exhalations of our houses turned to rubble? In these applications, the concept city represents, for example, soldering points, commodities in a department store, high-value military targets, job-shop schedules, or DNA fragments. By sending out colonies of virtual ant agents to arbitrage the differential kill geometries, we narrate the urban campaign in a fundamentally superpolynomial tense. Entering the cities, the guerrilla will regularize, just as amphibious gill-breathing hatchlings transform into fully lunged adults that consume the remaining larvae of social transformation. How then to coordinate except by mimesis of the market and its terrible imperatives the distribution of the go signal among the amplifying organs of the proto-instance? The trailers are most effective as barricades when flipped on their side and lit on fire; the simplest layouts are "the tooth" and "the garden" (see fig. 14). In modern cryptosystems, anonymity is simply the unbinding of the non-orientable plane of intimacy; the public a painful token that private individuals slip into each other's leaking spleen. I have heard the servers singing each to each, a song of massively large prime numbers crammed into the friendzone or driving up rent prices in the exurban commuter towns. The harassing forces should structure their attack like a good joke —an initial series of disorienting skirmishes and exchanges followed by a punchline that arrives when and where least expected.

The army and the people are one.
If this is correct, please press 1.
Every face that you see has a shame like a sun.
Is he one now? Is she one too?
From the towers, the deputies point and shout: *That one! That one!*
No one you know has been outside of the zone.

The army and the people are one.
I walked right into the house and turned it on.
A wall slid in front of the sun.
One plus one is one.
The risible boys and fungible girls
Build up their hungers into a facsimile of none.
The army blockades all the bridges, the tunnels.
Through loudspeakers, they tell us: the people have won.
You've had your fun, taking a hammer to the hard drive
In advance of the first waves of the Hun.
Little is known about the things we have done.

The army and the people are one.
But has anyone seen a people?
Was it holding a gun?
Do its movements coincide
With the price of bullion?

For those of us who lived through rebellion
What remains is Monday, mostly, Monday in abundance.
One taken away from one is one,
like Chronos eating his young.

A century is not so long.

The portent exfiltrates the meanings of the night. At the Holiday Inn Abyss, watching herself on cable news from the End of History suite, the last criminal gives it a doubtful look. We come quickly to the limits of the model world, as in the advertisements where the heroic automobile races toward the edge of a desert mesa, skidding to a stop yet imparting some of its momentum to the camera now wheeling over the abyss to track the flight of an imperious raptor who has little chance of surviving the impending collapse of regional ecosystem. Once it hits the aftermarket you'll pay ten times as much for an audience. You can take out the LA power grid with a well-placed shot from a .22, though in truth she is guilty of crimes that are far worse, infinite crimes the mere detailing of which by a court of law would serve as life sentence even for the immortals among us. Down there, working the burning coalface with a spoon, a saw, a drop-down menu containing thousands of words for time. How many will have died in their sleep, happily, of natural causes, to sustain this tiny and inconsequential perforation in the net of power? The last criminal, the first poet. If there was one, there were ten. If there were ten, there were twenty. We are not capable of time travel, says Maya, because we have yet to create the present. The last criminal is therefore given a slight reprieve, a pardon contingent upon the convocation of zeros in series. Exit King Lear. We watch his heat signature stumble about the dressing room on the giant screens set up in the square. Villon drives his dagger through the priest's ribs. The object of the heist, it turns out, is time itself—the beginning and ending of time, folded carefully within an unassuming lacquer box that contains enough computing power, we are told, to casually reorder the universe. The commandos rappel into the fossil record. The drum circle drowns out the assembly. You don't have to have a world to live in one.

Leveling up
through the smirking detail
relatable, as they say,
whither the general failing
of ordinary antiterror
to impede our movement
toward the equilibrium prices
at the back of the line
where we are quietly concussed
by a simple distribution matrix
for supercoordinate horror selfies
displayed on the sweatshirts of the victors.
The ground crawls into the sky.
Some guy wants money again:
artisanal pharmaceuticals lobbed into
a high window of the Villa Medici
just before everything gets fuzzed over
by Versace Medusa heads
at constant returns to scale.
The invertebrate jury, inveterate
defenders of the rights of the dead
to get dead, and stay that way, at any time
by virtue of the municipal
zoning laws designed to redirect

the flows of stored-up human
activity toward the processing stations.
They did that to our faces
while we were blindsided
by unforeseen mediocrity,
the airlock slowly filling up
with Prosecco, our unlikely heroes
swinging through the study
halls of the damned on psychotropic
lianas, as a pencil might accidentally
tear through the three-dimensional
commodity space like the discontinuity
introduced into a function
by the rebellion of a people
against their configuration as variable
quantities of corn, iron, sugar.
We keep examining
the hole in the world for news
about our true intentions
while our former students surf past
on subsistence vectors
that individuate them each to each.
They do not individuate me.

The sun crashes on the runway. There is no going back, says the fortune cookie. There is no going forward either, says the bill. The crank converts the linear, reciprocating motion of the caged steam into rotational energies whose appalling fires are distributed immoderately throughout the social organism by an elaborate maze of belts and pulleys. Arms horizontal, the child spins in place until he faints. They break up. They get back together. After three years of uncollected garbage, the government raises 4.2 billion on the bond market. A makeshift bomb explodes feebly outside the central bank, as if to congratulate the victors. You touch the arrow; crowds hurl themselves against the National Assembly. Cost per click finding its local minimum. The gravid melancholy of the river in the penstock, pushing into the kiloton rotors. Capital pours out of the country; when the economic refugees its flight produces finally arrive at their destination, it will have prepared a place for them. A filthy lather of pure means throbs above the sunken garden. The rotation of the sphere of the heavens, plotted on the flat plate. Joined end to end, electrical current effectively travels in both directions at once; almost everything that has ever been said or thought or meant now and for some indeterminate future floating out there as a mere momentary interruption of those signals, that needling tone. We can change course but it won't make a difference; at most, we can choose what part of the wall we want to hit. The centers take flight. The point becomes a line. The line becomes a plane. The plane becomes a time, repeating. Pulled around in a circle by the force of its name, the thing flies out against what it is, expelled by the disorder of its internal parts. The child steps forward from the huddled semicircle, the rock in his hand lobbed out into clear prose. From the rotation of the hips and shoulders, from the continuous turning into itself of verse, the first rock arcs out, then the next, then hundreds, thousands, darkening the sky, turning the sky to solid earth, to bedrock, the soldiers at the checkpoint buried under the thunder of it, the landslide. The marlin runs out all the line from the reel, snaps it. We drift through the burning city.

Inside the calorimeter, the everyday labor of the ordinary
laborers approximates bodily the aliquot
portion of the total social product
our faded scrip commands, oracles
whose average tediums model as weather
the trajectory of our lives, corkscrewing downward
through the terror-leveled visual heat
to become what we have or will have been,
calories and things, air and skin,
while the little dude folded inside
the parietal lobe gets lit up
by a hundred theoretical knees and elbows, row on row
of simulators for pulling, hauling, grinding, cutting, sorting,
with average methods, converting
the coordinated movements
into an abstract energy
that makes the giant's legs move
on an unmarked plane, in a manner of speaking,
as the giant has no body
and no continuous extension,
is perhaps not even a giant
but rather a swarm of dwarves
small enough to fit inside the
sliding cabinets of the things of this world,

where their controls panels are
easily accessible, though probably on fire
also, and feeding the boilers which eject
giant plumes of ethnographic steam
into selfsame futurity, governed
alternately by the deficits or surpluses
that send us careening along the interior edge
of a total hair care program
announced by a suite of designer ring tones
appropriate to the parlous
state in which we find ourselves
forced to unfriend everyone forever,
one counter-revolution colliding
with another in front of the state television
building without returning us to the regularly scheduled
programming of the status quo ante,
where our memories were prophecy
and our prophets, enemies.

To get born now is so much harder than it was at first, when there were just bodies and numbers, bodies and names, when the dead and the living were best friends. For one, the grammar is shit. You could end up becoming anyone, wobbled along the branching pulsions, the looped channels and weird maturities. It's not something you can just do to yourself, as you might for instance squirm free of the cheap, plastic handcuffs cops use for mass arrests. It takes years for the nervous system to suffuse the babyfat with reflexes adequate to the social belly but by that time it will already be too late. The transport van will have entered the transcontinental tunnel that carries the convicts to the outlands. You must, in other words, get born, in the same way that you might try to get a document notarized but find that you must first provide that selfsame notarized document as proof of eligibility. So long as this consciousness is lacking, the crisis is permanent, it goes back to its starting point, repeats the cycle until after infinite sufferings and terrible detours the school of history introduced by the enciphered transmission of genital imagery through the late-empire cellular networks allows for a single, perilous rendezvous far from the facial algorithms of the secret police. In the meantime you just sit there, a lump of nomination and triple cream, soliciting the indignities of the world on the basis of an entirely speculative kind of existence, stapled to the proverbial mountaintop while the fashionable and happy people swim up through your feed. Hours pass before the different subcommittees, working groups, commissions, and provisional departments are reconciled on the question of what, exactly, is going on. There is an object over there and you must retrieve it, though it has become increasingly impossible to reconcile the divergent viewpoints now present, sometimes vehemently so, within the meandering and inconclusive debate. Indeed, it is only by refusing the thudding recursions of the whistling machines and the motions they compel that the body might begin to displace larger and larger quantities of air, and therefore move, to everyone's surprise, toward its eventual goal of world communism. This might be total bullshit. I mean, something is here that was not here before, and no matter how many times you tally the inputs and outputs, their difference is not the half-shaped sound stuck in your throat, those jesting others, the plush plaids and swarming braids of total destroy. Something is here that was not here before. There's no more chorus. Only the people, armed, and the silvery rifts that snake through them. They are your mirror. They are what you would have been forever.

A child is dead. We ourselves are reasons.
Supersocial bees collect the liquid
directly from our flowering eyes.
The brew they make will wipe that dude
right off your face. A child is dead:
autotuned, the wailing sounds like joy,
like the total supply of blood
to every weird extremity of brain.
The marchers pass, trundling
their guillotine-soundsystem
down the fear-swept streets, heads
crowned with the gas mask of tragedy,
the balaclava of comedy,
behind which squirm and swim
the faceless headings of our age.
The city shuts off power to the block.
A child is dead. The world is reasons.
There was an error in the transit of the sun.
Bodies are being found and they are
not ours, approximately, yet truly.
Underneath, above, distance
blockades instance. We shout down the
sights, the light, all clocks, each why.

The dials palpitate in the smoke. On a screen the size of your eye and almost as close, humanized cats communicate our fundamental incapacity as humans to do anything about it. We're up to ten gigabytes per day. Their laughter has become, finally, the shadow of a word. From a tower in the historical record, the imprisoned Lollards are able to survey up and down the Thames the extent of their heresy. Men have become comfortable yelling their feelings into the face of a stranger. All along the walls of the dead, commentary drips into the psychic sump. There is no stopping these customers now; the overflow of cynics and their puerile synonymy will continue to rampage through our apartments, even after we have cut all power to the settlements by felling the utility lines with chainsaws and angle grinders, even after we have traveled from one end of the city to the other on a wheezing mule and restored water service to all the households that have been shut off for nonpayment. Like the panicked movement of a crowd, the tunnels fan out in every direction, distributed through the subsoil in the shape of indiscriminate obliteration. What we will remember about this planet, I think, is the knotted faces of the police, how many of them there were, on every corner, rummaging around in our closets when we came home, pulling the children out of school, how eagerly they reached for their weapons as the results of the probe came streaking across our screens. Out of the incubator and into the accelerator, pinballing among the lesser stars of the Orion Arm, I myself am hella....This whole weekend was a mistake. Like trying to use consciousness to explain what happened historically, a baby stroller jammed into an entryway of a squat and lit on fire, a composite of genital emotion and high theory now available in a single, easy-to-swallow pill. The smoke is sweet, oleaginous, sensitive to the vagaries of heart and mind, forming into particulate scripts that hover at the threshold of legibility, beneath which the conveniences of our decrepit age are burnt to cinders. The auctioneer looks into the security camera and clears his throat.

For once or for now
among the dank
postulates of invariance
new energies disorganize
the spray-tanned heirs
who contour the pure
whereabouts, that unreal urinal.
What is the value of gold
expressed as a quantity of gold?
I wouldn't really call that a tactic.
It's more like an instinctive
freakout redirected by ten
thousand years of bad vibes,
such that causes are briefly
relieved of all consequence,
the world destroyed and recreated
each instant, meaning there's
even less reason not to walk
right into the department store
and take whatever it is you want
while the great fear radiates
backward toward the capital
from the farthest market towns.
You can read off our occasionless

anthems from the velocity
memes of the bureaucratic layer
who tracked the poison
into every room of the castle,
who forgot who it was they
were trying to annoy.
Over the city the target
apertures abstract us
from embraces, as we hide
among the fungus of gears
in redevelopment alley
where the white allies
mutilate each other in sight
of the blind god of period style,
excess capacity wicked away from
the ring of failing business parks
by the poetry of currency,
the money absent from all earthly
money, as elsewhere the long
march through the luxury
hotels slows under the weight
of appropriated towels, toiletries,
minibar booze...

Our music had holes in it where what didn't happen could have and we passed through them, in supersonic fragments, rattling the cinders in the triumphal urn. You'll never hear it again and again like that again, its massified chords crashing through the hopeless plaza. In the courthouse, the prefecture, the post office: commerce of fire and interchange of fire. In the consulate, the legislature, the townhall: immediacy of fire and actuality of fire, returning to us as so much smoke and ash neither the fetters upon our own capacity to direct our lives as we saw fit nor the faked force staring out at us from the hole in the moon but that supple, liquid extension of our minds across the whole hyperplane of social possibility, burning now the Ministry of Intelligence, now the Department of Education, as if one might finally withdraw from the automatic teller not just the currency necessary to meet the week's obligations but also the wires and glass, the plastic buttons, the careful interlocking of bits and pieces that suffuses every inch of our social being. From the open windows of the Center for Humanities, incanting tongues of canvas spell out the divergent sum of demands, supplied from every direction by a contorted relay of human suffering. As such, when they finally ascend into the hanging valley above the River C, they find that the fabled cypress has been uprooted by the rage-drunk syndicate of river gods installed by the CIA in their war against Poseidon. In a dream that night she is told to cut a thin disc from the eight branch of the fifth branch of the third branch from the trunk read clockwise from the position of the sun at the moment of her awakening and place it upon a record player and follow, to the letter, the perilous instructions. The auxiliary police units take up their positions outside the mall, the gas station, the office park: Nothing can happen that has not already happened, they declare. We ask for proof, emphasizing the difference between a presentation of infinity and an operation upon it. At the center of the National Assembly, its roof largely removed by the bombs, truckloads of state paperwork carted out of the useless offices of the endless divisions of power fuel a supercomputing bonfire, symbol of the lawless and undetermined action of each person at every social point, no longer set against but in fact contingent upon the unrestricted action of all others. Whack-a-mole of immortals poking their heads up through the pores in the world, land and sky and sea stabilizing into a sunstruck parfait as the camera tumbles through space. Later, we would set out for the rumored northern wing of the mansion, splitting off from Balto-Slavic to link up with the Indo-Iranian corridor, the causeways through the void looping down beneath the magnetosphere in a grand figuration of something we no longer cared enough to remember. North, South, West: the branches of the chain stores flowering with the fires of life, the fluorescent matter.

Diagonally, by love and hate
in equal parts
propelled, the mob returns
like a chorus
the cops keep getting
hit with, in the head
brick and bottle tra la la
of *fuck you, pig* and *die, pig, die*

the mob, torn together
by each temporizing, tangled
moment in its series
returning along the old animal tracks
of total science to mark with metaphoric
shit and piss the places where the earth
parts ways with each reason for enduring:
its also-rans, its would-have-beens
crashing into the shatterproof
curves of the cell wall, behind which
the makers of measure and rule
shelter in disordered nomenclature,
recounting in pantomime
our unfortunate tenure
as minor villains among the plant life.

Just then, you feel the scare quotes
C-clamp your skull, interatomic
emoticons spazzing out intransitively
in the middle distance where demoralized
shifters replace all sense of the past
with continuously updated commentary
from the compliantly defiant crowds
who compare their purchases
with the bland openness of experience.

They will never be a real mob
now that nature has been democratized
by these marvelous poisons
our rounded-up truants
leave dusted upon the rocks and trees.
As for the rest of us, we learn
something important about ourselves
watching from the loading dock
as the mushroom cloud
announces the end of another season—
e.g., that each riot really is
an assemblage of other riots
washed up on the boulevards,
from whose faded corpses
one dresses and arms one's comrades
the total inadequacy of which
as equipment for the task at hand
traces out in negative
the seat perilous of the party historical
the poetry of the future
whose sweet new sounds
will fill with meaning slowly
while the seas rise.

Can software destroy hardware?
Can a class, acting strictly as
a class, abolish all classes
as the answer to a badly phrased
question might by sheer force of obviousness
cause the questioner to rise

blankly and walk into the ocean,
while the black flags cut from the robes
of executed magistrates
wave non-semaphorically,
where hope ends and history starts.

ACKNOWLEDGMENTS

Portions of this poem appeared previously in *Lana Turner, Try!, Everyday Genius, The Capilano Review, Hi Zero, Armed Cell, Dreamboat, Prelude, Tripwire*, and the anthology *It's night in San Francisco but it's sunny in Oakland*. The first 18 sections were collected in a chapbook published by Tenured Ninja in 2012. I am very grateful to the editors of these publications.

My poem takes its title from a patch of graffiti that appeared on the wall next to a looted jewelry store after a minor riot in Santa Cruz, California. The phrase rings a change upon a difficult-to-translate line of Eugène Pottier's original French lyrics for "The Internationale," *Nous ne sommes rien, soyons tout!* Many English-language renditions leave the line out, but Charles Hope Kerr's version translates it as "We have been nought, we shall be all." The quoted language on page 12 is from Hegel's *Phenomenology of the Spirit* (¶545). The prose section on pages 18-19 borrows from *The Journal of Eugène Delacroix* and Thomas Carlyle's *History of the French Revolution*. The question in the final stanza of the poem is adapted from Theorie Communiste's description of the central problematic that communist inquiry and practice must confront (see the text "Who Are We?").

The first section of this poem originated with notes from a long walk that Tim Kreiner and I took among the foreclosed houses of Berkeley and Oakland in the summer of 2008, while the economic crisis was still incipient. From these scribbled beginnings to the very last edits, the project has been enabled by friends like Tim. Anne Boyer read every word many times over, and offered crucial advice, as well as a recommendation that lead to the prose section on pages 72-73. Joshua Clover has been a collaborator and accomplice throughout the years of composition, and nearly every page owes something to our work together. The section on pages 61-62 is dedicated to Tim Simons and the one on page 65 to Maya Gonzalez. I am also particularly grateful to Chloe Watlington for her help with printing, to Juliana Spahr for her incisive edits, and to Chris Nealon and Margaret Ronda for encouraging articles about early versions. Finally, the writing of this book would have been both impossible and meaningless were it not for the love and good counsel of Anna Shapiro as well as the continuous example of our wonderful children, Noah and Astrid. These names are but a tiny fraction of the many people—friends, comrades, strangers—who contributed to this work, directly or indirectly.